Y0-EKC-117

MAPLE VALLEY BRANCH LIBRARY
1187 COPLEY ROAD
AKRON, OHIO 44320
330-864-5721

MAR 0 5 2010

Grandparents Raising Kids

THE CHANGING FACE OF MODERN FAMILIES

Adoptive Parents
Blended Families
Celebrity Families
Families Living with Mental
& Physical Challenges
First-Generation Immigrant Families
Foster Families
Gay and Lesbian Parents
Grandparents Raising Kids
Growing Up in Religious Communities
Kids Growing Up Without a Home
Multiracial Families
Single Parents
Teen Parents
What Is a Family?

Grandparents Raising Kids

Rae Simons

Mason Crest Publishers, Inc.

Copyright © 2010 by Mason Crest Publishers. All rights reserved. No part of this publication may be reproduced or transmitted in any form or by any means, electronic or mechanical, including photocopying, recording, taping, or any information storage and retrieval system, without permission from the publisher.

MASON CREST PUBLISHERS INC.
370 Reed Road
Broomall, Pennsylvania 19008
(866)MCP-BOOK (toll free)
www.masoncrest.com

First Printing

9 8 7 6 5 4 3 2 1

ISBN 978-1-4222-1496-1
ISBN 978-1-4222-1490-9 (series)
Library of Congress Cataloging-in-Publication Data
Simons, Rae.

Produced by Harding House Publishing Service, Inc. www.hardinghousepages.com
Interior Design by MK Bassett-Harvey.
Cover design by Asya Blue www.asyablue.com.
Printed in The United States of America.

Although the families whose stories are told in this book are made up of real people, in some cases their names have been changed to protect their privacy.

Photo Credits

Albert Anker p. 37, Peter Harrison p. 50, Hasan Sami Bolak p. 42, Carmen Gordilla Rojas p. 53, Georgios Iakovidis p. 17, Mattes p. 54, Ranveig p. 18, Seidenstud p. 41, Brian Harrington Spier p. 56, Sigismund von Dobschütz p. 27, Ansgar Walk p. 38

Contents

Introduction   6
1. Going to Grandma's House   8
2. Growing Up with Two Mothers   15
3. Growing Up with Grandpa   25
4. Raising Grandchildren   34
5. Abuelita   49
Find Out More   59
Bibliography   61
Index   63
About the Author and the Consultant   64

GRANDPARENTS RAISING KIDS

Introduction

The Gallup Poll has become synonymous with accurate statistics on what people really think, how they live, and what they do. Founded in 1935 by statistician Dr. George Gallup, the Gallup Organization continues to provide the world with unbiased research on who we really are.

From recent Gallup Polls, we can learn a great deal about the modern family. For example, a June 2007 Gallup Poll reported that Americans, on average, believe the ideal number of children for a family to have these days is 2.5. This includes 56 percent of Americans who think it is best to have a small family of one, two, or no children, and 34 percent who think it is ideal to have a larger family of three or more children; nine percent have no opinion. Another recent Gallup Poll found that when Americans were asked, "Do you think homosexual couples should or should not have the legal right to adopt a child," 49 percent of Americans said they should, and 48 percent said they shouldn't; 43 percent supported the legalization of gay marriage, while 57 percent did not. Yet another poll found that 34 per-

Introduction

cent of Americans feel a conflict between the demands of their professional life and their family life; 39 percent still believe that one parent should ideally stay home with the children while the other works.

Keep in mind that Gallup Polls do not tell us what is right or wrong. They don't report on what people should think—only on what they do think. And what is clear from Gallup Polls is that while the shape of families is changing in our modern world, the concept of family is still vital to our sense of who we are and how we interact with others. An indication of this is the 2008 Gallup poll that found that three out of four Americans reported that family values are important, while one in three said they are "extremely" important.

And how do Americans define "family values"? According to the same poll, here's what Americans say is their definition of a family: a strong unit where faith and morals, education and integrity play important roles within the structure of a committed relationship.

The books in the series demonstrate that strong family units come in all shapes and sizes. Those differences, however, do not change the faith, integrity, and commitment of the families who tell their stories within these books.

7

GRANDPARENTS RAISING KIDS

1 Going to Grandma's House

Terms to Understand

sociologists: people who study human beings and how they interact with each other and form groups.
epidemics: things that occur suddenly, spread quickly, and affect a large number of people.
incarceration: being put in prison.
vulnerable: able to be hurt.
internalize: to take an idea or emotion and make it personal.
baby boomer: someone born during a time of increased birth rates, especially those born after World War II, between 1946 and 1965.

Traditionally, families go to their grandparents' home for holiday meals; children may spend special weeks in summer at Grandma's house. For many children, Grandma's house is the place where you get spoiled. But nowadays, that's changing. More and more children are going to their grandparents' house—to stay.

Between 1980 and the end of the twentieth century, the number of children living with their grandparents increased by nearly 50 percent. By 2000, more than 4 million American children were being raised by grandparents. Five years later, that number had climbed to 6 million, about one in every eight children.

Sociologists say this recent trend in American families is caused by a number of factors. These include the public health *epidemics* of drug abuse, teen pregnancy, HIV/AIDS, and violence. Divorce and *incarceration* are

1 • Going to Grandma's House

also factors that contribute to grandparents needing to step in and raise their children's children.

Raising children is not easy for grandparents at a time in their lives when both their energy levels and income have gone down. Young children require a level of care

In earlier generations, grandparents were often members of the household. They helped with childcare while receiving the support they needed from their own children. In today's society, however, the generations are less likely to live together.

GRANDPARENTS RAISING KIDS

President Barack Obama (shown here as a young man with his grandmother at his high school graduation) is a good example of someone who lived with a grandparent during part of his growing-up years. He credits his grandmother with teaching him and inspiring him—but he also recognizes that she had biases and prejudices typical of white women of her generation.

that can be exhausting, and grandparents who take on this responsibility often find their health suffers as a result. Caregiving grandparents may also feel overwhelmed and depressed; they may feel lonely and isolated from others their own age; they may not know where to turn for help. And when they made their financial plans for their old age, they probably weren't counting on raising another set of children.

Grandparents raising their children's children also face legal issues. Since they are responsible for their grandchildren's medical care, schooling, and other care aspects, they need to have the legal authorization to make needed decisions. Otherwise, authorities may view them as simply babysitters and deny them the rights and assistance they need

1 • Going to Grandma's House

(such as health insurance). The legal arrangements that can be made by grandparents raising their grandchildren are adoption, guardianship, foster-parent status, and caregiver's authorization. Seeking to adopt a grandchild can be financially expensive—and it may be emotionally draining as well, since it often puts grandparents at odds with their child, the parent of their grandchildren. Adoption is the most secure and stable outcome for the children, though.

> Researchers have found that grandparents raising children are more *vulnerable* to a wide range of problems that include depression, loneliness, poverty, and poor health.

Going to live with their grandparents can be difficult for the children as well. Even if their parents were abusive, children usually miss them and mourn their loss. The children's mixed-up emotions can lead to emotional and behavioral problems that can range from very mild—such as acting out at school—to very serious—such as suicide. These kids often need counseling; they may also need other special services in a school setting.

Meanwhile, the grandparents are dealing with their own emotions. They would not be in this new role if the family had not already been seriously damaged. If their children have been incarcerated, are physically or mentally ill, or are abusing drugs, grandparents will feel worried; they may feel guilty and hold themselves responsible for the way their children have turned out. If the children have died, grandparents may be struggling with a heavy load of grief.

The grandparents' other children—the aunts or uncles of the grandchildren—may also have to deal with a range

GRANDPARENTS RAISING KIDS

> Experts have found that care-giving grandparents are 50% more likely to have problems getting around and doing the tasks of daily life than non-care-giving grandparents.

of emotions. They may feel jealousy that the "problem child" is getting more of their parents' attention and financial resources than they are. If they have children of their own, they may feel that the grandchildren who live with the grandparents are the favorites.

But it's not all bad! The grandparents who shared their stories in this book also report that their grandchildren have brought new life and love into their lives. Grandchildren say they have benefited from their grandparents' care and wisdom.

According to the book of Peter in the Christian New Testament, "love covers a multitude of sins." Ultimately, a family is simply a group of people who love each other and who do their best to care for each other. No family is perfect—but love helps "cover" the failures and imperfections.

HEADLINES

(From "I Love You, Grandma-Mom!" by Janie Sullivan, *Looking for Clues*, January 13, 2006, www.bkserv.net/LFC/article.aspx?ArticleID=46#Article)

I remember my grandparents. Vaguely. . . . We only saw them once a year for about a week when we were kids. After we grew into teenagers and then young adults, we did not see them that much. Grandpa died first, then five years later Grandma followed him.

1 • Going to Grandma's House

All my friends had grandparents that lived far away. Grandparents they saw once in a while. I do not remember my grandparents having jobs; in fact, I did not know what my grandfather did for a living until many years after his death. My grandmother did not work outside the home. She raised eight children. I wonder what she would think about me being a grandmother. She might not understand why my three-year-old granddaughter lives in my house without her mom or her dad. In fact, my grandmother would probably be shocked that my granddaughter does not even know who her father is and that her mother is in jail.

I am a **baby boomer**, a single mother of three, a single grandmother of seven, and one of the growing group of grandparents who are raising their grandchildren. My daughter, who spent most of this pregnancy (her second) in jail, delivered a beautiful baby girl. . . . I was in the delivery room with her and was the first person to hold the baby. The father had not really ever been in the picture, and he certainly was not at the hospital that day. He has his own family somewhere else and is not interested in this baby.

Little Trinity is three now, and her mother is back in jail, the second time since Trinity was born. The last time she was arrested, I went to court and applied for legal guardianship. I needed to make sure Trinity

> Grandparents raising children is more common in inner cities, where between 30% and 50% of all children are in the care of grandparents.

GRANDPARENTS RAISING KIDS

was taken care of, and there was no one to care for her but me. . . .

Some friends and even family members tell me they don't understand why I am doing this. They say I don't have to, that there are programs that will take care of Trinity if her parents cannot or will not. They sometimes resent the fact that I don't have time for socializing anymore, or that any social activities I do take part in must include Trinity. They may be right, but I know that I could not do anything else. I don't want to say I don't have any other choice, because I do. However, I have made the only choice I know how to make: to take care of Trinity for as long as I need to. And when she wraps those little arms around my neck and whispers, "I love you, Grandma-mom," it is all worth it. I think my Grandmother would agree.

> When grandchildren come to live with their grandparents, boys are more apt to act out their emotions with external behaviors, while girls are more likely to *internalize* their upset feelings.

What Do You Think?

Do you think most grandparents today have different roles than they once did? What about your grandparents? How involved in your life are they? Do you think the author of this article is unusual? Why or why not? How do you think Trinity will feel about her grandmother when she is older?

2 • Growing Up with Two Mothers

2 Growing Up with Two Mothers

Daniel lives in a house full of women: his thirty-six-year-old mother, his seventy-seven-year-old grandmother, and his ninety-four-year-old great-grandmother. When Daniel was small, Nona, his great-grandmother was the one who played games with him, who sang him songs, who made him laugh. Mom was the one who bought him presents and took him on outings. And Grandma was the one who cooked his meals, washed his clothes, scolded him, and put him to bed. Daniel lived in the same house with his mother—but from the time he was born, his grandmother was the one who raised him.

When Daniel was very small, he never minded all the women in his life, but as he entered his teen years, he wished more and more often that he was not the only male in the household. "Nona's so old now, all she does is sleep, and I really miss her," he says. "She was the

> **Terms to Understand**
>
> **aerobic exercise:** exercise that makes the body use more oxygen; for example, anything that involves running or moving quickly.
> **anaerobic exercise:** exercise such as weight lifting that builds muscles through tension, instead of by using more oxygen.

GRANDPARENTS RAISING KIDS

In 2000, 4.1% of white, 6.5% of Hispanic, and 13.5% of black American children lived with their grandparents.

happy one in our house. Now it seems like my mother and grandma fight all the time. Sometimes they drive me crazy. It's always noisy at my house. I don't really mind, most of the time, but some days I just want to yell, 'Shut up, everyone, please!'"

What makes it harder for Daniel is that his mother and grandmother mostly fight about him. His grandmother has lots of experience raising young children but not much understanding of twenty-first-century adolescents—so it's no wonder she and her daughter don't see eye-to-eye on how to raise Daniel. It's especially hard for the older woman since while Daniel was younger, her daughter had stepped back from any child-raising responsibilities. "Grandma was in charge when I was a little kid," Daniel says. "So she thinks she should still be the one who decides what I do and don't do, where I go, what I wear. Now that I'm older, though, my mom makes some of the decisions about what I do and don't do, and she wants to be more involved in my life. But then she and Grandma don't agree. So there's lots of screaming around here."

Daniel doesn't always know what's okay for him to do and what's not. "My mom says some things are okay—like she doesn't have a problem with me wearing certain clothes or taking the bus by myself when I want to go places. But my grandma throws a fit if she sees me wearing things she says makes me look like a gangster. So I mostly just stuff what I'm really going to wear at

2 • Growing Up with Two Mothers

school into my book bag, and then I put it on once I'm out of the house. And I don't tell Grandma what I'm doing after school or on Saturdays. Mom and I have this kind of secret agreement that we just don't tell Grandma the things that would upset her. We lie to her all the time, but we know that keeps her happier." But then there are other things that Daniel's grandmother permits that his mother won't. "Like my grandma doesn't care what I eat. She'll cook me whatever I want and let me eat as much as I want—but my mom is always worrying that I'm too fat and getting on my case. And if I go to the store with Grandma, she'll buy me whatever I want, stuff that

This nineteenth-century painting shows that more than a hundred years ago, grandmothers were also involved in their grandchildren's discipline.

17

GRANDPARENTS RAISING KIDS

It is common in many cultures for a grandmother and a mother to share the responsibilities of child raising.

my mother would say I didn't need. Same thing with homework—Mom wants me to get better grades, but Grandma says the school gives me too much work and that a kid deserves to have free time in the evenings. So if Mom's out, I don't do my homework, because Grandma doesn't care—but if Mom's home, then I do."

Things were simpler for Daniel when he was younger, he says. "Then it was like I just had to listen to Grandma.

2 • Growing Up with Two Mothers

She was the one I really counted on from day to day. It's funny how things can change, though. She seems so *old* now. I still love her a lot, but it's hard to take her as seriously as I used to. 'Specially since I know my mom really doesn't pay attention to what Grandma thinks. Not at this point anyway. But sometimes I feel sorry for Grandma. She doesn't feel good a lot of the time, and I know she gets sad after she and my mom fight. But it's her fault. She's the one who starts the fights usually. So I guess I'm kind of mixed up. I mean I feel bad for my Grandma and I love her. But I'm not sure what I'm supposed to be doing different."

In the summers, Daniel spends a week with his mother's brother, his uncle Joey. He enjoys the chance to get away from all the arguing at his house. "Sometimes I wish I could go live with Uncle Joey. But he has kids of his own. He says I need to stay with Mom and Grandma."

Daniel doesn't think things will ever change, not while he still lives at home. "Even though my mom fights with my grandma, my mom knows that Grandma's getting older. She needs Mom, even if she won't admit it. And my mom probably couldn't afford to pay rent, so it's good we live here together. I just gotta live with it, I guess."

One of Daniel's favorite memories is going to a Native American demonstration with his uncle Joey and his family. "I got to talking with one of the guys

> About one in ten grandparents will raise a grandchild at some point in the child's life for at least six months—and usually for three years or more.

19

there who was showing us how his people made a dug-out canoe. I told him I lived with my mother, and he said that his people believe that a man who is raised by his mother grows up strong and wise. So I guess I'm going to be double-strong and double-wise when I'm a grownup—because I pretty much have two mothers."

HEADLINES

(From "Promoting Healthy Lifestyles Among Grandparents Raising Grandchildren" by Chutima Ganthavorn and Joe S. Hughes, *Journal of Extension*, February 2007, vol. 45, no. 1.)

During 2003–2004, a . . . project was designed to work with both grandchildren and grandparents, aimed at reducing obesity by a two pronged approach: 1)increasing fruit and vegetable consumption and 2)increasing physical activity.

Recruitment efforts were targeted at youth ages 9–12 from households where grandparents are raising grandchildren. . . . All families were low income. About 55% received federal assistance, and 44% were below 150% poverty level. When asked whether they ran out of food before the end of the month, 72% answered "sometimes" or "always." Grandchildren participating in this project had been living for a

2 • Growing Up with Two Mothers

relatively long time with their grandparents (4–12 years), and in most cases grandparents were their legal guardians.

. . . A total of 11 grandparents and 12 grandchildren filled out the survey at the start of the project. The majority of grandparents (91%) and grandchildren (83%) indicated that they had seen the food guide pyramid. (This project was conducted in 2004, before the introduction of MyPyramid). . . . All grandparents and 75% of grandchildren knew that what you eat can increase your disease risk. The same number of grandparents and grandchildren also believed that overweight people are more likely to have health problems. But only 36% of grandparents and 33% of grandchildren believed that underweight people are more likely to have health problems than appropriate weight people.

The majority of grandparents (82%) believed that most people their age think eating fruits and vegetables every day is a very good thing to do. However, when asked about their family's opinion, only 45% of grandparents thought people in their family believe eating fruits and vegetable every day is a very good thing to do. The results were just the opposite for grandchildren. Only 50% of grandchildren believed that most people their age think eating fruits and vegetables every day is a very good thing to do. But

Grandparents raising grandchildren has become more common in recent years in Canada as well as in the United States.

GRANDPARENTS RAISING KIDS

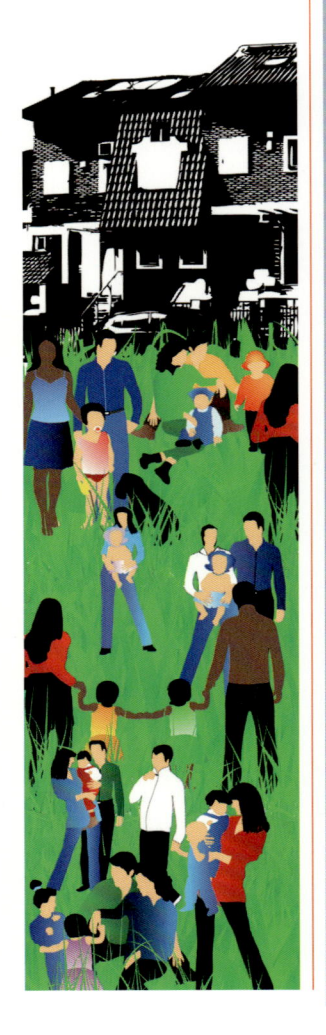

more children (67%) thought people in their family believe eating fruits and vegetables every day is a very good thing to do.

Participants were asked to estimate their fruit and vegetable consumption during the past week. Eighty percent of grandparents and 62% of grandchildren reported that they consumed 100% fruit juices, like orange juice, apple juice, or grape juice, less than three times during the last 7 days. About the same numbers of grandparents (82%) and grandchildren (62%) consumed fruit less than once per day. Seventy-three percent of grandparents and 80% of grandchildren ate a green salad less than 3 times during the past seven days. Sixty-four percent of grandparents and 60% of grandchildren ate other vegetables like carrots less than once per day.

When asked whether they ate two or more servings of vegetables at their main meal, only 27% of grandparents answered "Always." Ten percent of grandparents said they always eat fruit or vegetables as snacks. Twenty percent of grandparents always used Nutrition Facts on the food label to help choose foods.

The majority of grandparents (80%) watched 3+ hours of television on an average day. Less than half (42%) of grandchildren reported that they

2 • Growing Up with Two Mothers

watched 3+ hours of television on an average day. When asked how many days during the past week they spent at least 20 minutes doing *aerobic* exercise, 82% of grandparents and 33% of grandchildren said 3 days or less, and more than half (55%) of grandparents said 1 day or less. A larger number of grandparents but a lower number of grandchildren participated in *anaerobic* activity. About 54% of grandparents and 59% of grandchildren said they spent 3 days or less during the past week doing a minimum of 30 minutes of anaerobic activity. Almost all of grandparents did not do any strength training during the past week. About 91% grandparents said they spent 0-1 day on strength training during the past week. About half of grandchildren reported that they spent 3 days or less on strength training.

Sixty-three percent of grandparents and 42% of grandchildren said they rarely or never exercise with their family. Fifty-five percent of grandparents and 67% of grandchildren said their families encourage them to exercise often or every day.

The survey established that there was a great need for change in health and nutrition habits of grandparents raising grandchildren.

GRANDPARENTS RAISING KIDS

What Do You Think?

Put in your own words the main ideas reported in this article. Do you think that problems with diet and exercise are more or less likely to occur in households headed by grandparents? Why? Do you think any of the information reported in this article plays a role in Daniel's life? What evidence from Daniel's story makes you think this?

3 Growing Up with Grandpa

There are many children being raised by their grandparents together or by their grandmothers alone; not so many being raised by their grandfathers alone. But that's what happened to Melody James.

"When my parents died in a car accident when I was baby," Melody says, "my grandfather stepped in with one hundred percent commitment. If he hadn't, I don't know what would have happened to me. For as long as I can remember, he was my mother, father, and best friend, all rolled into one."

Her grandfather was sixty-five at the time and already caring for a wife who was dying from cancer. "To this day people at church tell me how surprised they were when they saw how my grandfather took care of me. He'd been the kind of guy who hunted and fished while

Terms to Understand

fixed income: when a person brings in the same amount of money every week, month, or year.
tolerant: having a fair and accepting attitude about different beliefs, ideas, and customs.
introvert: a person who is quieter and more focused on his or her own thoughts.
extrovert: a person who is more outgoing and tends to be focused on things outside him- or herself.
social worker: someone whose job involves working with those who are struggling with serious illness, poverty, or other difficulties and helping them improve their conditions.

GRANDPARENTS RAISING KIDS

> Grandmothers are nearly seven times more likely to be raising grandchildren than are grandfathers.

his wife did the housework. But he took care of me like it was the thing that made him the happiest in the world. He was the most loving parent I have ever seen, and I consider myself to be tremendously lucky. From the moment I came to live with him, he let me know I was the most important person in the world to him."

Melody's grandmother died while Melody was still very young, so she grew up without any women role models. "When I was about six, I had this big hero worship thing going for Madonna. It worried my grandfather. He talked to me a lot about Grandma, about what a gentle person she'd been, about how she acted and dressed. I can't say I paid a lot of attention when I was young, but I think I absorbed the stories without realizing it. Now that I'm older, I think about Grandma and imagine how she would handle my life or how she would advise me if she were still alive."

Melody's grandfather was already retired when she came to live with him, so he had plenty of time to devote to his young granddaughter. "He was always fixing something or volunteering to help someone with something, and he'd bring me along with him. I grew up knowing how to hammer nails and use a drill. I think those are just as important skills as using a sewing machine or baking cookies."

But her grandfather's retirement also meant he lived on a **fixed income**. "I didn't realize it at the time," Melody says, "but I see now that we didn't have much money.

3 • Growing Up with Grandpa

While it's true that more grandmothers are involved with raising grandchildren than grandfathers, some older men are very capable of taking on the responsibilities and joys of child raising.

We ate a lot of macaroni and cheese and frozen dinners, and I didn't have as many toys as a lot of kids my age, and I never had all the clothes other little girls did. But I didn't really care. Those things never seemed all that important to me."

GRANDPARENTS RAISING KIDS

The famous children's story of Heidi and her grandfather is a literary example of a grandfather successfully raising his granddaughter.

Melody believes that who she is today is in large part due to her grandfather's influence on her life. "Grandpa was a gentleman. He always spoke softly, and he always treated me with respect. From him, I learned that everyone is valuable, everyone deserves kindness. He was old-fashioned in many ways, but he was still **tolerant** of the new generation. Most of all, he was always there for me—at every school event, at all my basketball games when I got older, at every awards banquet. He was never too tired or too busy. He helped me with my homework, played checkers with me after supper, took me out to lunch after church on Sundays. I loved being with him."

Despite how much she loved him, Melody admits she went through a rebellious phase when she was a teenager. "I horrified him when I got a tattoo on my neck. He didn't approve of how much makeup I wore or the way I dressed, and I know he didn't like the kids I hung

3 • Growing Up with Grandpa

out with for a while there. I guess I had to prove that as much as I loved him, I still had to be my own person. He was so calm, so conservative, an *introvert*—and I was this jumpy teenager, a thrill-seeker, an *extrovert*."

Today, though, Melody feels she becomes more like her grandfather the older she gets. "I think about him a lot, every day, and I consciously strive to become more like him. When he died, he left an enormous hole in my life. I think that's the biggest drawback of being raised by a grandparent—they have to leave you too soon, before you're ready to be all on your own in life. They're not going to be there to see your children. But I like to think my grandpa is still watching over me, my own personal guardian angel."

> Nearly twice as many black American grandparents as white grandparents are raising children.

What Do You Think?

Despite how nice her grandfather was, why do you think Melody went through a "rebellious phase"? Compare Melody's experience to Daniel's. What explains the differences between their families? What do you think Melody's life would have been like if she'd been raised by both her grandmother and grandfather? Or only her grandmother instead of her grandfather?

29

GRANDPARENTS RAISING KIDS

HEADLINES

(From "Grandparents Raising Grandchildren" by Pauline Gordon, *Gotham Gazette,* April 2006, www.gothamgazette.com/article/children/20060412/2/1816)

When my grandmother was trying to raise my sister and me, she faced many hardships. At times it seemed as if she and I were coming from two completely different worlds. We rarely agreed on anything and ended up in a lot of arguments. But then my grandmother had to go to a hospital, and then my sister and I had to move to a regular foster home. It was very clear to me that, whatever the conflicts and complications, it just feels much better to live with relatives than strangers.

In fact, a number of experts have solid evidence that kids who can't live with their parents do better in homes with relatives. Studies show they have fewer behavioral problems and less chance of abuse. This is why New York State passed a law in 2004 saying that grandparents must be informed whenever a child is put in foster care, so that they might be able to step forward and look after the child themselves. The law also makes it easier for grandparents to gain legal custody of grandchildren they're already raising. . . .

Although experts say that this influx of kids into their grandparents' homes is preferable to traditional foster

3 • Growing Up with Grandpa

care, they also note that social services is still playing catch up. Elderly caregivers face a host of unique challenges that too often go unmet, as they did with my grandmother. . . .

But New York City has become a pioneer in addressing the challenges of grandparent caregivers, by opening the nation's first housing complex specifically for grandparent-headed families,

Grandparent Family Apartments, a six-story apartment building on Prospect Avenue in the South Bronx opened a year ago, the nation's first public development exclusively for grandparents raising grandchildren. The families living in the 51 apartments all get a *social worker*, support groups and parenting classes. Children receive tutoring and organized activities in the afternoon and evening. Apartments also have special amenities for the elderly—like cords you can tug on if you need help.

Annie Barnes, 62, one of its residents, has lived in the building since it opened. Like many grandparent caregivers, Barnes never expected to be a parent at her age. But 11 years ago she found herself raising her two grandchildren after her son was murdered. "When I turned 50 I wanted to do things for myself and travel places. I had to put my plan on hold to provide for my grandchildren," she said.

> About a third of all grandparents raising children are younger than 55 years old; another third are between the ages of 55 and 64, and another third are over 65.

GRANDPARENTS RAISING KIDS

Both Barnes' grandchildren, Alonzo Poinsett and Shakela, had been born prematurely and with serious health problems. She needs a lot of help raising them, but living in the trailblazing apartment complex, she says she can swing it.

Dorothy Jenkins, 76, also lives in the Grandparent Family Apartments. She got custody of her grandchildren when her daughter died. "There was no other alternative," she said, meaning she refused to let them be put in foster care. So she retired to raise her grandchildren full-time. "I had to start all over again," she said, adding that she's a strict parent.

In her old home Jenkins used to worry about safety. Now she says she feels secure. "You know what I'm doing right now?" she said. "I'm in bed, watching TV, while my front door is open—and I'm not worried. It's a great life for me."

Although both women said, "These children need to stop running up and down the stairs!" they were more than satisfied with their new apartments.

Grandparents Raising Kids